NOTES ON IQBAL'S ASRAR-E-KHUDI

(The Secrets of the Self)

Edited by :

Arthur J. Arberry

KITAB BHAVAN
New Delhi-110002 (INDIA)

Kitab Bhavan
1784, Kalan Mahal, Darya Ganj
New Delhi-1100 02
Phone : 91-11-23277392/93, 23274686
Fax : 91-11-23263383
Email : nasri@vsnl.com
Website : www.kitabbhavan.com

Edition 2005

ISBN : 81-7151-364-6

Laser Typesetting at :
T.J. Enterprises
Pataudi House, Darya Ganj,
New Delhi-1100 02 (India)

Published by :
Nusrat Ali Nasri for Kitab Bhavan
1784, Kalan Mahal, Darya Ganj,
New Delhi-1100 02 (India)

Printed in India at :
Lahooti Fine Art Press
1711, Suiwalan,
New Delhi-1100 02 (India)

Preface

After Professor R. A. Nicholson's death in 1945 his library was sold to a well-known Cambridge book-seller. As I was looking through the volumes offered to the public, I chanced upon a copy of his translation of Iqbal's Asrar-e-Khudi, in the first edition (London, 1920), and was immediately interested to observe that this copy was heavily corrected and annotated, in a hand other than the translator's. On studying the character of the notes, it seemed likely to me that these (and of course the corrections) emanated from no other than Sir Muhammad Iqbal himself. This supposition was strengthened when I found a few lines of dedication in a copy of one of his publications which he had sent as a present to Professor Nicholson. Probability at last became a certainty when I shewed the book to Mr. Javid Iqbal, who is at present studying with me in Cambridge. He confirmed that the corrections and annotations were indeed in the handwriting of his revered father.

Meanwhile I had compared this corrected copy with the revised translation issued at Lahore in 1940 (reprinted 1944), and found that all the changes made by the translator in that edition were based upon Iqbal's notes. I discovered furthermore that some of Iqbal's most interesting notes had not been included, as these threw light upon important aspects of his philosophy, and illuminated his poetic art, it seemed highly desirable to collect and edit them. At the same time it would be instructive to draw up a list of all the passages where corrections had been made, so as to indicate the nature of these corrections and the exact relationship between the first and second editions of Professor Nicholson's translation.

The most arresting fact which emerged from the study of this new material was the extreme difficulty of reaching a correct interpretation of many passages in Iqbal's poetry. Professor Nicholson was at the height of his great powers when he made his translation of the Asrar-e-Khudi; it was shortly after the completion of this task that he began work on the Mathnawi of Jalaluddin Rumi, a labour which occupied the rest of his life and crowned his splendid achievements in the field of oriental studies. All who put their hands to translating Iqbal may therefore well feel humbled, when they consider how many times the inner sense of his poetry escaped Professor Nicholson's deep and careful scholarship. But they may well rejoice, that fortune has preserved this unique example of Iqbal's exegesis of his own writings, by studying carefully the material which is assembled in these pages, the future worker in this field will find much to assist his undertaking.

I have used the symbol N. to indicate the first (1920) edition of Professor Nicholson's translation. The letter I. is appended to all the corrections and annotations in Sir Muhammad Iqbal's handwriting. The phrase Cf. N. rev. invites the reader to compare the changes and additions made in the second (revised) edition of the translation. The material marked I. is printed exactly as it occurs in the original copy, including erasures.

Arthur J. Arberry

Introduction

Page xx. "The true person not only absorbs the world of matter; by mastering it he absorbs God Himself into his Ego." N.

"The true person not only absorbs the world of matter by mastering it; he absorbs God himself into his Ego by assimilating Divine attributes." I.

Page xxiv. "... as the Qur'an peaks of a barzakh, or intermediate state, which lasts until the Day of Resurrection." N.

"... as the Qur'an speaks of a barzakh, or intermediate state, which, in the case of some individuals, will last until the Day of Resurrection." I.

Translation

Line 5. "The Gardener taught me to sing with power." N.

"The Gardener tested the power of my song." I.

"The Gardener tried the power of my song." N. rev.

Line 6. "He sowed a verse and reaped a sword." N.

"He sowed my verse and reaped a sword" I. Cf. N. rev.

Line 13. "My thought hunted down and slung from the saddle a deer." N.

"[a deer] *i.e.* a new theme." I.

Line 16. "Full-blown roses are hidden in the skirt of my garment." N.

"The flower hidden in the twig *i.e.* unborn flowers of ideas are in the skirt of my garment." I.

"Unborn roses are hidden in the skirt of my garment." N. rev.

Line 18. "I smote the heartstrings of all that heard me." N.

"I smote the string of the life-vien (*sic*) of the universe." I

"I smote the heart-string of the universe" would perhaps be a better rendering." I. Cf. N. rev.

Line 24. "Not yet is my quicksilver astir."' N.

"[quicksilver] (*i.e.* sunshine)." I.

Line43. "How many a poet after his death . . ." N.

"The idea is that some poets are not understood or appreciated in their lifetime. They are, so to speak, born after their death, and spring up from their graves like roses from dust." I.

"Many a poet was born after his death," I. Cf. N. rev.

Line 46. "When roses blossomed o'er the earth of his grave " N.

"Like roses blossomed o'er the earth of his grave" I.

"Like roses blossoming o'er the earth of his grave." N. rev.

Line 71. "The old Guru of the Sky taught me this lore." N.

"This word Guru does not seem to be quite appropriate, پیر گردوں is heaven. Persian poets love to call it پیر *i.e.* old. I think it wouldbe sufficient to say—" Heaven taught me this lore." I. Cf. N. rev.

Line 76. "Were it a beggar, a king would pay homage to it." N.

"If a beggar worship it (*i.e.* liqour [*sic*]) he would become a king." I.

"Were a beggar to worship it, he would become a king." N. rev.

Line 94. " And sprinkle the dry herbs with my tears." N. "آب در کاه کردن is a Persian idiom— The practice of herb-sellers is to sprinkle water over their herbs so that they may fetch more money by making them heavier. The idea is that I may exalt the worth of poesy by putting the soul's deepest longings into it (poetry) آب چشم *i.e.* tears stands for the longings of the soul." I. Cf. N. rev. p. 8 n.l.

Line 97. "His soul is the source of the flames." N.

"His soul is a despository [*sic*] or bed of flames." I.

"His soul is the flaming furnace." N. rev.

Line 102. "And clothed my barren dust with beauty." N.

"Out of my cold dust he built flames, *i.e.* his poetry has fired up my soul." I.

"And set my ashes aflame." N. rev.

Line 105. "I am a wave and I will come to rest in his sea." N.

"I am a wave and come to rest in his sea." I.

Line 108. "Will draw life from the breath of his words." N.

"Live by the aid of his breaths *i.e.* he sustains my spritual [*sic*] life." I.

"Draw life from the breath of his words." N. rev.

Line 116. "Who wrote the Qur'an of Persia." N.

"Who rendered the Qur'an in Persian." I. Cf. N. rev.

Line 120. "Dash thine head against the cupping-glass and thine eye against the lancet!" N.

"شیشه is here the goblet of wine not, the cupping-glass. Dash the goblet against thy head (break it) after thou hast drunk the contents, and dash thine eye against the lancet—so that you may be relieved of the intense heat within thy soul." I.

"Dash thine head against the goblet and thine eye against the lancet! " N. rev.

Line 127. "Like the bell, break silence at last, and from every limb." N.

"'Like the bell, break silence at last, and from thy material frame of clay ' would perhaps be better." I.

Line 134. "Break the bottles in the bazaar!" N.

"شیشه برسر بازار شکستن is an idiom which means to disclose the secret." I.

Line 135. "Like the reed-flute, bring a message from the reeds." N.

"نیستان *i.e.* Being a part bring a message from the whole." I.

"Like the reed-flute, bring a message from the reed bed." N. rev.

Line 136. "Give to Majnun a message from Laila!" N.

"Give to Majnun a message from the tribe of Laila." I. Cf. N. rev.

Line 138. "Enrich the feast with thy piercing strains!" N.

"بزم is, I think, assembly. Feast conveys a slightly different idea." I. Cf. N. rev.

Line 168. "I am a breath, yet am I sprung of fire." N.

"Literally—" Though I am nothing more than smoke, yet I am born of fire' *i.e.* though my poetical merit is small, I have spiritual kinship with the great poets of Islam." I.

"I am but smoke, yet am I sprung of fire." N. rev.

Line 170. "Cast abroad the secret of this veil.;' N.

"Cast abroad the secret behind this veil." I. Cf. N. rev.

Line 193. "By the Self the seed of hostilit is sown in the world." N.

"[the seed of] opposition (In the Hegelian phrase—' contradiction')" I. Cf. N. rev.

Line 208. "The fragrant navel justifies a hundred musk-deer." N.

"One fragrant navel justifies a hundred musk-deer." I. Cf. N. rev.

Line 210. "The suffering of moths is justified by the candle." N.

"The idea is that the beauty of the candle-flame is a sufficient excuse for the suffering of the moths. The evolution of perfection must involve suffering. We must, therefore, in the words of Nietzsche, say yae (*sic*) to the sufferings of life. Schopenhauer did not appraise suffering properly." I.

Line 215. "Subject, object, means, and causes—" N.

"Subject, object etc. are categories of thought, necessitated by action. It is possible that life will invent or evolve other categories when the sphere of its action changes. The literal translation of the verse is —' The self transforms itself into subject, object etc. for the purposes of action.'" I.

Line 216. "They all exist for the purposes of action." N.

"*i.e.* in the present sphere." I.

"All these are forms which it assumes for the purpose of action." N. rev.

Lines 231-2. "Power that is unexpressed and inert

Chains the faculties which lead to action." N.

"The Self is a power hidden and yearning for activity and since its life is action it imprisons itself in the means to action, *i.e.* it individualises itself so that action may become possible." I.

Line 235. "When a drop of water gets the Self's lesson by heart." N.

"The drop of water as drop has only an unstable individuality; when it hardens itself into a pearl it reaches a higher stage in individuation." I.

Line 243. "But the wave, so long as it remains a wave in the sea's bosom." N.

"The wave, *i.e.* so long as it remains a distinct individual." I. Cf. N. rev.

Line 245. "Light has been a beggar since the eye first rolled." N.

"Literally — 'Light transformed itself into a circle (*i.e.* individualised itself) until it (light) became an eye; it is the impulse for the enjoyment of beautiful sights that made the eye move *i.e.* quickened it into life. The idea is that desire determines the evolution and character of our organs.'" I.

"Light transformed itself into an eye." N. rev.

Line 247. "But for as much as the grass found a means of growth in its self." N.

"The grass, when it found an impulse for growth from its deepest self its aspiration etc." I.

"When the grass found a means of growth in its self." N. rev.

Line 257. "Because the earth is firmly based on self-existence." N.

"Because the earth is firmly based on its self." I. Cf. N. rev.

Line 261. "The glory of the plane fixes our gaze." N.

"چنار is a majestic tree abundantly found in the valley of Kashmir. Its leaves are red like fire." I.

"The glory of the red beech fixes our gaze." N. rev.

Line 274. "The nature of every thing is faithful to desire." N.

"The nature of every thing is despository [*sic*] of desire." I.

"The nature of everything is a storehouse of desire." N. rev.

Line 280. "And when it takes life, all dies that is not true." N.

"And when it takes life, all but Truth dies." I.

Line 281. "When it refrains from forming wishes." N.

"When it refrains from forming desires:" I. Cf. N. rev.

Line 283. "Desire is ,an emotion of the Self." N.

"The ceaseless uproar of the Self is due to desire." I.

"Desire; keeps the Self in perpetual uproar." N. rev.

Line 285. "Desire is a noose for hunting ideals." N.

"Desire is a noose for hunting objects." I.

Line 286. "A binder of the book of deeds." N.

"*i.e.* introduces orderliness into the chaos of human action." I.

Line 288. "Even as absence of burning extinguishes the flame." N.

"Even as absence of heat extinguishes the flame." I. Cf. N. rev.

Line 293. "Away from the reed-bed, the reed became happy." N.

"*i.e.* Transplanted from the reed-bed the reed achieved a distinct individuality of its own and the result of this separation is that it sent forth music. Its music is due to its isolation (attainment of individuality)." I.

Line 295. "Why does the mind strive after new discoveries and scale the heavens?" N.

"What is the essence of the mind which strives after new discoveries and scales the heavens?" I. Cf. N. rev.

Line 298. "And the intellect is a child of its womb." N.

"And the mind is a child of its womb." I. Cf. N. rev.

Line 301. "A desire which broke through by its own strength." N.

"A desire which realised itself by its own strength." I. Cf. N. rev.

Line 305. "All these are weapons devised for self-preservation." N.

"All these are weapons devised by life for self-preservation." I. Cf. N. rev.

Line 306. "By him that rides into the battle of Life." N.

"In its ceaseless struggle." I. Cf. N. rev.

Line 310. "Science is a means of establishing the Self." N.

"Science is a means of invigorating the Self." I. Cf. N. rev.

Line 314. "The lines following this line up to 'last day' qualify ideal." I.

Line 315. "If thou art an ideal, thou wilt shine as the dawn." N.

"An ideal, shining as the dawn.' I. Cf. N. rev.

Line 316. "And be to all else as a blazing fire." N.

"A blazing fire to all that is other than God." I. Cf. N. rev.

Line 317. "If thou art an ideal, thou art higher than Heaven." N.

"An ideal higher than Heaven. I. Cf. N. rev.

Line 334. "The Fountain of Life is Love's flashing sword." N.

"Love is the fountain of life as well as the flashing sword (*i.e.* death)." I.

"Love is the Fountain of Life, Love is the flashing sword of Death." N. rev.

Line 337. "Learn thou to love, and seek to be loved." N.

"Learn thou to love, and seek a beloved." I. Cf. N. rev.

Line 354. "The sanctuary of the Ka'bah is his dwelling place." N.

"His dwellingplace is a sanctuary to the Ka'bah itself." I. Cf. N. rev.

Line 363. "In the hour of battle, iron was melted by his sword." N.

"In the hour of battle, iron was melted by the flash of his sword." I. Cf. N. rev.

Line 365. "When he was called to aid, his sword answered 'Ameen'." N.

"When he prayed for Divine help his sword said Ameen i.e. His prayers were followed by personal effort." I. Cf. N. rev.

Line 378. "He covered her face with his own veil." N.

"ردا is چادر some other word such as mantle would perhaps be better. Viel [*sic*] is used in the preceding line." I. Cf. N. rev.

Line 386. "He gave to Makkah the message, 'No blame shall be laid upon you'." N.

"He gave to Makkah the message, 'No punishment shall be laid upon you.' These words were uttered after the conquest of Makkah." I.

"He gave to Makkah the message, 'No penalty shall be laid upon you'." N. rev.

Line 412. "And reaped a harvest of delight." N.

"And reaped a harvest of sight. If we sow eyes we ought to reap sight or vision. (Vision is perhaps better than sight)." I.

"And reaped a harvest of vision." N. rev.

Line 421. "From the wine of Love spring many qualities." N.

"From the wine of Love spring many states of the soul." I.

"From the wine of Love spring many spiritual qualities." N. rev.

Line 422. "Amongst the attributes of Love is blind devotion." N.

"تقلید is following the other without any personal exercise of reason. The idea is that تقلید is also a form of love." I.

Line 434. "And interpret to thee the text..." N.

"And make thee the object of the text 'Lo, I etc.'" I. Cf. N. rev.

Line 446. "And ride like children on a woman's back ?" N.

"And ride like children on a reed ? (In the East children love to ride on sticks. Cf. طفل نی سوار" I. Cf. N. rev.

Line 458. "Seek not waves of water from the fountain of the sun." N.

"Seek not water from the fountain of the sun, *i.e.* Do not seek the bounty of the rich." I. Cf. N. rev.

Line 479. "The beggar's wallet is like a boat tossing in waves of fire." N.

"A whole ocean if gained by begging is a sea of fire. The idea is that a self-earned drop of dew is better than a borrowed ocean." I.

"A whole ocean, if gained by begging, is nothing but a sea of fire." N. rev.

Lines 493-4. "The reference in this verse is to the Masnavi of Bu 'Ali beginning with the couplet—

مرحبا ای بلبل باغ کهن

از گل رعنا بگو باما سخن I.

Line 498. "The wine of Bu 'Ali's discourse had turned his head." N.

"Inebriated with Bu'Ali's love-potion." I.

Line 534. "Of a majesty that was firm as a mountain." N.

" Of a kingdom that was firm as a mountain. The idea is that by one little song the poet saved a kingdom." I. Cf. N. rev.

Line 556. "And sought by craft to restore his fortunes." N.

"And sought by craft to restore the fortunes of his race." I. Cf. N. rev.

Line 557. "The weak man, in order to preserve himself." N.

"The weak, in order to preserve themselves." I. Cf. N. rev.

Line 558. "Seeks devices from skilled intelligence." N.

"Seek devices from skilled intelligence." I. Cf. N. rev.

Line 633. "His Pegasus went astray in the darkness of philosophy." N.

"His Pegasus went astray in the darkness of ideality." I.

"His Pegasus went astray in the darkness of idealism." N. rev.

Line 634. "And galloped over the mountains of Being." N.

"And lost its hoof in the rocky valley of actuality. hoofless- افکنده سم" I.

"And dropped its shoe amidst the rocks of actuality." N. rev.

Line 635. "He was so fascinated by the Ideal." N.

"He was so fascinated by the invisible." I. Cf. N. rev.

Line 636. "That he made head, eye, and ear of no account." N.

"That he made hand, eye, and ear of no account, *i.e.* the senses were untrustworthy according to Plato." I. Cf. N. rev.

Line 640. "His cup sends us to sleep and takes the world away from us." N.

"His cup sends us to sleep and deprives us of the sensible world." I.

"His cup sends us to sleep and takes the sensible world away from us." N. rev.

Line 644. "He called the world of phenomena a myth." N. "And called the world of phenomena a myth." I. Cf. N. rev.

Line 663. "Our philosopher had no remedy but flight." N.

"Our hermit (or Ascetic) had no remedy but flight (from the real world)." I.

"Our recluse had no remedy but flight." N. rev.

Line 670. "I know not whether it is the dregs or the bricks." N.

"I know not whether it is the dregs or a brick of the wine-jar. The story in the East is that Plato had to hide himself in a jar. Cf. خشت خم . خم افلاطون is brick placed beneath or over the wine-jar. In either case his phantasy is worthless." I. Cf. N. rev.

Line 671. "The peoples were poisoned by his intoxication." N.

"Whole peoples were poisoned by his intoxication." I.

Line 672. "He slumbered and took no delight in deeds." N.

"He slumbered and took no delight in action." I.

Lines 699-700. "Ere tulips blossomed in his brain.

There was heard no note of joy or grief." N.

"Unblossomed tulips.

And unheard notes of joy and grief grow in his brain (soul). The idea is that the poet's soul is full of original themes." I.

Line 704. "He creates beauty in that which is ugly and strange." N.

"He creates beauty and knows not what is ugly." I. Cf. N. rev.

Line 715. "But when his zephyr blows in our gardens." N.

"When his zephyr blows in our garden." I. Cf. N. rev.

Line 716. "We stay loitering amongst tulips and roses." N.

"Slowly does it steal into the tulips and roses." I.

"It slowly steals into the tulips and roses." N. rev.

Lines738-42. "He takes from thy soul the desire of existence,

He extracts from thy mine the blushing ruby.

He dresses gain in the garb of loss,

He makes everything praiseworthy blameful.

He plunges thee in a sea of thought,

And makes thee a stranger to action." N.

"He takes from thy soul the desire of existence,

Extracts from thy mine the blushing ruby,

Dresses gain in the garb of loss,

Makes everything praiseworthy blameful,

Plunges thee in a sea of thought,

And makes thee a stranger to action." I.

Line 767. "Thy ill-usage hath paled his cheek." N.

"Thy illness hath paled his cheek." I. Cf. N. rev.

Line 792. "It behoves thee to go back to the Arabs," N.

"It behoves thee to go back to Arabia." I. Cf. N. rev.

Line 793. (footnote), "refers to the Qur'an and the ideals for which it stands." N.

"refers to purely Muslim ideals in Literature and religion." I. Cf. N. rev.

Line 833. "The wind is enthralled by the fragrant rose." N. "The flower-prison turns air into fragrance *i.e.* the air becomes fragrance by being pent up (restrained) in the flower-bud. The idea is that restraint leads to perfection." I.

"The air becomes fragrant when it is imprisoned in the flower-bud." N. rev.

Line 834. "The perfume is confined in the navel of the musk-deer." N.

"The perfume becomes musk when restrained in the navel of the musk-deer." I.

"The perfume becomes musk when it is confined in the navel of the musk-deer." N. rev.

Lines 861-2. "The mixing of clay with water nourishes the body.

But he that is drowned in sin dies an evil death." N.

"The mixture of water and clay *i.e.* man is ease-loving.

Enamoured of evil and lover of what is bad." I.

"Man, in whom clay is mixed with water, is fond of ease,

Devoted to wickedness and en-amoured of evil." N. rev.

Line 869. "Whoso dwells in the Muslim Faith." N.

"Whoso dwells in the world of Negation. لا is the first word of the کلمه. لا stands for negation; الا for affirmation. This is Sufi phraseology." I. Cf. N. rev.

Line 875. "The profession of Faith is the shell, but prayer is the pearl." N.

"The profession of Faith is the shell, and prayer is the pearl within." I. Cf. N. rev.

Line 881. "The pilgrimage enlightens the minds of the Faithful." N.

"The pilgrimage enlightens the soul of the Faithful." I. Cf. N. rev.

Line 906. "He will bring another world into existence." N.

"He brings another world into existence." I.

Line 907. "A hundred worlds like this world of parts and wholes." N.

"A hundred worlds like this world of part and whole." I.

Line 931. "He bestows life by miraculous works." N.

"He bestows life by his miraculous action." I. Cf. N. rev.

Line 932. "He founds a new system to work by." N.

"He renovates old ways of life." I. Cf. N. rev.

Line 941. "When our handful of earth has reached the zenith." N.

"Our handful of earth has reached the zenith." I. Cf. N. rev.

Line 942. "That champion will come forth from this dust!" N.

"For that cavelier [*sic*] will come forth from this dust!" I.

"For that champion will come forth from this dust." N. rev.

Line 943. "There sleeps amidst the ashes of To-day." N.

"There sleeps amidst the ashes of our To-day." I. Cf. N. rev.

Lines 963-4. "When thou art there, we will lift up our heads,

Content to suffer the burning fire of this world." N.

"It is to thee that we owe our worth. And silently undergo all the pains of life.

The idea in these lines is that the promise of the perfect man justifies all the painful evolution through which humanity is passing. The idea is fully worked out in The prolegomena (1) p. 171.200." I.

"It is to thee that we owe our dignity.

And silently undergo the pains of life." N. rev.

Line 966. "The idea of the line is that the personality of Ali constitutes the very faith of Love *i.e.* Love holds him as dear as a man would hold his faith." I.

Line 975. "This was the habit of the Prophet.

It is recorded that the Prophet did so several times." I.

Line 996. note. "A miracle of the Prophet." N.

"A miracle attributed to 'Ali. This miracle is known as رجعت آفتاب I. Cf. N. rev.

Lines 999-1000. "خیبر شکن and قسیم کوثر are also names of 'Ali." I.

Line 1003. "The reference in this line is to the Tradition of the Prophet — انا مدینة العلم وعلی بابها I. Cf. N. rev.

Line 1013. "If thou art unfit to be either a wall or a door." N.

"If out of your own earth you da not build your own wall or door etc." I.

"Unless from thine own earth thou build thine own wall or door." N. rev.

Line 1023. "To comply with this ill-starred world." N.

"'نامساعد' is unfavourable to one's purposes and ideals. These lines controvert Spencer's definition of life—Life is adjustment to surroundings. The idea is that the powerful man does not adjust himself to his surroundings ; it is the surroundings that have to adjust themselves to his temperament. Adjustment to surroundings is a tacit confession of defeat in the battle of life." I.

"To comply with the world which does not favour thy purposes." N. rev.

Line 1036, "It is true life to give up one's. soul." N.

"*i.e.* If it is not possible to live in a manly fashion then it is better to die like men." I.

"Then it is better to die like a He-man." N. rev.

Line 1037. "He that hath sound intelligence." N.

"He that hath a sound heart." I.

" He that hath sound heart." N. rev.

Line 1039. "Tis sweet to use love in hard tasks." N.

"Tis sweet to love hard tasks." I.

Line 1043. "Mean spirits have no weapon but spite." N.

"Mean spirits have no weapon but resentment." I. Cf. N. rev.

Line 1044. "This is their one rule of life." N.

"Life has only one law (The law of life is mentioned in the following line)." I. Cf. N. rev.

Line 1045. "But Life is power made manifest." N.

"Life is power made manifest." I. Cf. N. rev.

Line 1047. "Mercy out of season is a coldness of Life's blood." N.

"*i.e.* shows poverty, of life." I

"Merey out of season is a chilling of Life's blood." N. rev.

Line 1054. "Its milk is a fattening for vices." N.

"On its milk vices fatten." I.

"Vices fatten on its milk." N. rev.

Lines 1057 sqq. "All the pronouns refer to weakness for which "Its" is used in the preceding lines." I. Cf. N. rev.

Line 1063. "Sometimes he is disguised as a victim of oppression." N.

"Sometimes it is disguised as compulsion." I. Cf. N. rev.

Line 1064. "Sometimes as one whose sins are to be excused." N.

"Sometimes as excusableness." I.

"Sometimes as excusability." N. rev.

Line 1071. "The false claimant, if he be possessed of power." N.

"A claimant, if he be possessed of power. I. Cf. N. rev.

Line 1080. "I have already written to you about this expression ["Be a tyrant!"] The allusion is to the Qur'anic verse — انه كان ظلوما جهولا I.

Line 1106. "Love has allied mercy with, wrath." N.

"جلال and جمال are the Sufi expressions. Cf. (Beauty and Power; Pen and Sword)." I.

"Love had allied beauty with majesty." N. rev.

Line 1111. "When the stone was anxious on account of the glass." N.

thought

"When the stone believed itself to be a glass *i.e.* when the powerful think themselves to be weak, they become weak." I. Cf. N. rev.

Line 1117. "Why be angry with mighty men ?" N.

"Why be angry with friends ?" I.

Lines 1207-8. "Thou art a condensed wavelet of smoke,

Endowed with the properties of a single spark." N.

"A condensed wavelet of smoke, Endowed with a single spark.

These two lines indicate the gist of the soul's being." I. Cf. N. rev.

Line 1249. "The Sheikh laid the seal of silence on his lips." N.

"The Brahmin laid the seal of silence on his lips." I. Cf. N. rev.

Line 1250. "Then he said: "O wanderer in the lofty sky." N.

"Then said the Shaikh: "O wanderer in the lofty sky." I. Cf. N. rev.

Line 1289. "O born of the womb of the revolving sky." N.

"According to Hindu belief Ganges comes from the sky." I.

Line 1290. "A fallen-in bank is better than thou." N.

"The sense of this line is not clear. A person fallen on the bank of the river (*i.e.* unable to walk) is better than thou (who art able to walk—*i.e.* immobility who is better [than] the movement which leads to self-effacement." I.

Line 1294. "Do not go to the florist in order to smell sweet!" N.

"Do not go to the Plucker of flowers in order to spread thy fragrance !" I.

"Do not go to the florist in order to spread thy perfume !" N. rev.

Line 1316. "Let it complain of the straitness of thy skirts !" N. "Let it complain of the straitness of its skirts !" I. Cf N. rev.

Line 1325. "*i.e.* In his will is lost the Will of God—whatever he does is the doing of God." I.

Line 1328. "In the world he is a witness against mankind." N.

"In the world he is a witness to mankind, *i.e.* The life of the true Muslim reveals to mankind the ideal realised ; it is thus a witness to all mankind. In this verse there is an allusion to the verse of the Qur'an—

"وكذالک جعلنا كم امتاً وسطاً لتكونو شهدآءً

على الناس ويكون الرسول عليكم شهيدا

I. Cf. N. rev.

Line 1329. "His high estate is attested by the Prophet that was sent to men and Jinn—" N.

"His high estate is attested by the Prophet—sent to men and Jinn—" I.

"His high estate is attested by the Prophet who was sent to men and Jinn—" N. rev.

Line 1330. "By the most truthful of witnesses." N.

"The most truthful of witnesses." I. Cf. N. rev.

Line 1332. "Shed the light of God o'er the darkness of works!" N.

"Shed the light of God o'er the darkness of thy deeds!" I. Cf. N. rev.

Line 1348. footnote. "Aurangzib." N.

"Shahjahan." I. Cf. N. rev.

Line 1374. "His culture lays a wide land waste." N.

"تعمیر is building *i.e.* for the sake [of] one building he lays waste a whole world." I. Cf. N. rev.

Line 1376. "His empty-headedness, and his oppression of the weak." N.

"It is owing to his empty-handedness that the [*sic*] oppresses the weak (*i.e.* to extort money from them)." I.

"His empty-handedness causes him to plunder the weak." N. rev.

Line 1395. "Thou hast being, and art thou afraid of not-being?" N.

"Thou art being, and art thou afraid of not-being ? (*i.e.* death)" I. Cf. N. rev.

Line 1396. "O foolish one, thy understanding is at fault." N.

"O dear one, thy understanding is at fault. The words ای سرت گردم in the original show affection ای سرت گردم- May I go round thy head; may I be a sacrifice for thee!" I. Cf. N. rev.

Line 1436. "It will not brighten the glass of thy

perception." N.

"It brightens the glass of perception." I. Cf. N. rev.

Line 1442. "And clean consumed the book of philosophy," N.

"And clean consumed the library of the philosopher." I. Cf. N. rev.

Lines 1483-4. "Having fire, it is yet cold as the tulip;

Having flame, it is yet cold as hail." N.

"Its fire is cold like tulip-flame; its flames are as cold as hail." I.

"Its fire is cold as the flame of the tulip;

Its flames are frozen like hail." N. rev.

Line 1500. "His mosque is consumed by the Christian monastery." N.

"His mosque is consumed by the monastic spark." I. "His mosque is consumed by the sparks of monasticism." N. rev.

Line 1522. "And ignoring their religious duties." N.

"Insensible of the great needs of Islam." I. Cf. N. rev.

Line 1528. "And the mufti of the Faith sold his decision." N.

"And the mufti of the Faith sold his verdict." I. Cf. N. rev.

Line 1531. "Green be the pure grave of Shafi'i." N.

"Green be the honoured grave of Shafi'i." I.Cf. N. rev.

Line 1536. "All its brilliance is derived from Life." N.

"In its water (edge) there is life." I.

"In its flashing edge there is life." N. rev.

Lines 1547-8. "The revolution of the sky is visible,

The change of day and night is perceived." N.

"The revolution of the sky (*i.e.* Time) is worth seeing ; the chang of day and night is worth discerning,*i.e.* Turn your attention to the nature and meaning of Time." I. Cf. N. rev.

Line 1555. "Thou mak'st this line a girdle on

thine infidel waist." N.

"زنار- a girdle. Perhaps 'thread' is better. This thread is 'worn by infidels." I.

Line 1559. "Art thou a Muslim ? Then cast off this-girdle." N.

"Art thou a Muslim ? Then cast off this thread." I.

Line 1566. "Life is a part of the contents of Time's consciousness." N.

"Life is one mystery [*sic*] among the mysteries [*sic*] of Time." I.

"Life is one of Time's mysteries." N. rev.

Line 1580. "لا تسبو الدهر ان الدهر هوالله —Do not abuse Time, for Time is God." Cf. N. rev.

Line 1595-6. "A new age hath been endued with our beauty

And hath risen from the dust of our feet." N.

"The new age with all its glories.

Hath risen from the dust of our feet." I. Cf. N. rev.

Line 1608. "We are the preservers of the

universe." N.

"We are the protectors of the universe." I. Cf. N". rev.

Line 1615. "Our essence is the mirror of the Divine essence." N.

"In our essence Divinity is mirrored." I. Cf. N. rev.

Line 1623. "Once more let us hear thy call to honour." N.

"Once more demand from us the sacrifice of name and fame." I. Cf. N. rev.

Line 1635. "When the people let the clue of Unity go from their hands." N.

"When the people of Islam let the thread of Unity go from their hands." I. Cf. N. rev.

Line 1643. "We are travellers : give us devotion as our goal!" N.

"We are travellers : give us resignation as our goal!" I. Cf. N. rev.

Line 1645. "*i.e.* Negation." I.

Line 1646. "*i.e.* Affirmation." I. Cf. N. rev.

Line 1656. "But my secret thoughts have not escaped from my heart." N.

"But none ever sought the secret thoughts within my soul." I. cf. - N. rev.

Line 1661. "A flame that seized the furniture of judgement." N.

"A flame that burnt to ashes the wares of Understanding." I. Cf. N. rev.

Line 1662. "And cast fire on the skirt of discretion." N.

"Cast fire on the skirt of discretion." I. Cf. N. rev.

Line 1663. "And lessoned with madness the reason." N.

"Lessoned Proud Reason with madness (of Love)." I.

"Lessoned with madness the proud reason." N. rev.

Line 1664. "And burned up the existence of knowledge." N.

"And inflamed the very being of knowledge." I. Cf. N. rev.

Line 1671. "At last flames breathed from every hair of me." N.

"At last flames grew up burst forth from every hair of me." I. Cf. N. rev.

Line 1675. "Is the breast of this age without a heart?" N.

"The breast of this age is without a heart." I. Cf. N. rev.

Line 1676. "Majnun trsmbles lest Laila's howdah be empty." N.

"Majnun is pained because Laila's howdah is empty." I.

"Majnun quivers with pain because Laila's howdah is empty." N. rev.

Line 1695. "There is dancing in every nook of the wine-house." N.

"There is dancing in every nook of the wilderness." I. Cf. N. rev.

Line 1698. "Thou hast decked out for Thy self a whole world." N.

"Thou hast created— evolved for Thyself—a whole world *i.e.* in order to relieve thy solitary Unity." I. Cf. N. rev.